Jaimee Nix is a coal miner's daughter from Seaham, County Durham. She is a retired teacher of engineering and product design, living in the South East of England. A gifted acapella singer and poet who uses her talents to share the history of the North East and her observations of life in general.

Her poems and songs are performed at folk clubs and acoustic music venues and are enthusiastically received.

Due

Blessings

Jaimee

Nix

To Jan Pearce
who gave me the push to start this journey.

Jaimee Nix

LAMENT FOR MY HOMETOWN

AUSTIN MACAULEY PUBLISHERS®

LONDON • CAMBRIDGE • NEW YORK • SHARJAH

A CIP catalogue record for this title is available from the British Library.

ISBN 9781035883769 (Paperback)
ISBN 9781035883776 (ePub e-book)

www.austinmacauley.com

First Published 2025
Austin Macauley Publishers Ltd®
1 Canada Square
Canary Wharf
London
E14 5AA

Adele Carne, my niece, also a miner's daughter, for her photographic skills.

Ray Lonsdale for his sculptures which portray the culture and history of the N.E.

Beamish the Living Museum of the North.

Table of Contents

A Miner's Life

Aye wor miners, but we have a life
S'not all dark and dingy, trouble and strife.
There's Geordie with e's whippets
Which he runs and races Sundays

There's Ron whose got e's pigeons
he flies them every day
an'e's got one that's a champion.
The fastest blue and grey.

They're in a Cree on his allotment,
we've all got one of them.
It's where I grow me veggies
and keep some ducks and hens.

I've also got me darts,
I'm a regular at the club.
A working men's that is,
not the same as a regular pub.

Friday night there's music
and snooker in the hall.
There's Bingo and the slot machines
and always the fresh meat draw.

There's Fred who loves his fishing
down the beach or off sea wall.
Generally catching Mackerel,
more often nowt at all.

Not forgetting the football pools.
The rep comes every Thursdy,
I even tried to spot the ball
but now A' do the lottry.

It's a good life while we're young and fit
and hope to retire well.
But some are not so lucky,
If the dust makes breathing hell.

Aberfan

If I mentioned Merthe Vale
you'd only know it was in Wales,
it has a story, oh so sad,
of a village, called Aberfan.
> Mistakes were made, and lessons learned,
> another page of history turned.

It was rain-sodden ground
where underground rivers were found.
Many warnings were ignored
and every day the waste was poured.
> Mistakes were made, and lessons learned,
> another page of history turned.

More than 90 years of mining waste
tipped out on the mountainside.
There was no time to warn them
when the slurry starts to slide.
> Mistakes were made, and lessons learned,
> another page of history turned.

The hooter sounded much too late
under desks the children hid.
It could have been a drill,
but that was a mistake.
     Mistakes were made, and lessons learned,
     another page of history turned.

The slurry slipped so swiftly down
that underneath the children drowned.
116 children gone.
We keep their memory and sing this song.
     Mistakes were made, and lessons learned,
     another page of history turned.

     At 09.15 h on 21 October 1966, a coal slag heap collapsed
on to a primary school in the mining village of Aberfan, South
Wales, killing 116 children; 145 children survived.
     In civil engineering, the word tip became official in 1971.
Landslip and flow slides still happen around the world.

Down Below

Death is waiting down below
Down below where the miners go.
Their sweaty backs breaking cutting coal.
Death is waiting down below.

Fire's been smouldering down below
Down below where the miners go.
A fire that's got nowhere to go
Except to break out down below.

That fire did break out down below
Down below where the miners go.
Low main caught fire in 1964
Men had to fight it down below.

To seal the fire off down below
Down below where the miners go.
They sandbagged the entrance, one more to go.
To seal the fire off down below.

The last bag going in down below
Down below where the miners go.
could cause a vacuum and make it blow
Killing the miners down below.

The seams now walled up down below
Down below where the miners go. But
the fire's still burning behind that wall
And miners work on down below.

This is the true story of Seaham colliery. My father (James
Marchant) was the deputy and safety officer who had to go
down and supervise the closure of the seam. He explained the
process to me when I was older. I remember the pit siren
going off in the night. I was 10 years old at the time. My dad
said that coal can smoulder for many years because some
oxygen seeps down through the strata. Sometimes there is
enough oxygen buildup to make it flame. It is only when it
meets a gas pocket that explosions can happen. The last
sandbag blocking the seam can cause a vacuum, but the
suction doesn't necessarily put the fire out.

From a Candle on a Hat

From a candle on a hat,
to a torch and battery pack,
brightening the gloom and the dark.
They once used canaries, now they use the Davey lamp
keeping miners safe from the deadly fire damp.
Just to go deeper and further underground
to where what we're after can be found.

It was Welsh mined gold, made
the late queen's wedding ring am told.
And starting with a spade or a pick
Miners dug tunnels under no man's land,
doing their wartime bit.

For lead, it's up ladders to a parapet,
where even there, conditions are wet.
Watch out those below!
When the pick gets a grip
with a wrench and heave ho!
The whole lot comes tumbling down.

So, whether it's tin, lead, gold, or coal
men have mined with their body, mind, and soul.
Many men were killed, and many got sick
machines made things easier than a shovel and a pick.

Yet, today the arguments continue to goad
saying fossil fuel is wanted no more!
No investment puts more men on the dole.
The riches are still there in the ground
where open-cast mining or quarries abound.
Shall we rip open the countryside?
or dig neath the soil?
We're already riddled from centuries of toil.
There's still Tin in Cornwall and Cumbrian coal,
Tungsten in Devon and some Scottish Gold.

One day in the future will their history shine,
will they send men or robots to dig the new mines?

Lead/Galena is found in vertical veins.

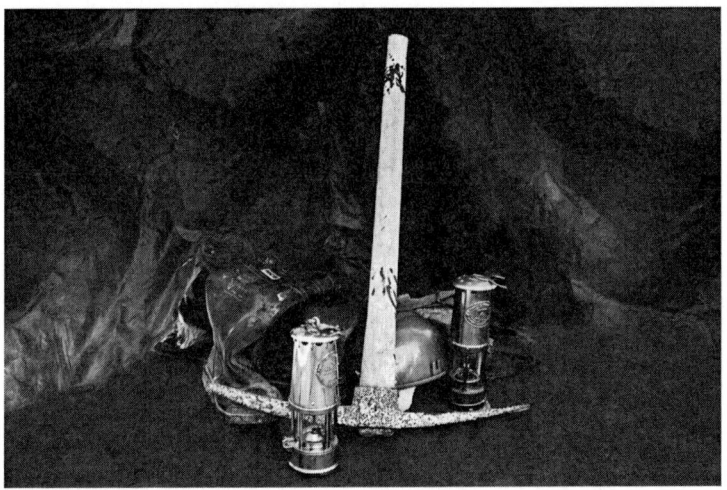

Geordie's Wake

Hale and Hearty shout and cheer,
drinking scotch or drinking beer.
Hale and hearty lads and lasses
drinking wine in fancy glasses.

Drink to those who're lost and gone
remembered well in rhyme and song.
Hale and hearty raise a tankard
raise a flagon or raise a glass.

Swing your arm don't spill a drop
let comrades know they're not forgot.
Speak their name and give a cheer,
another round, another beer.

Play the music, feel the beat
laugh and dance and stamp yer feet.
Hug a partner, shake a hand,
enjoy this time of feeling grand.

Hale and hearty another barrel.
Open another bottle or two.
Those of us who are still standing,
have really only had a few.

Hale and hearty Geordie's wake.
Not going home until its late.
Hale and hearty singing songs.
Goodnight! Farewell to everyone.

Grace Darling

The Forfarshire on a stormy night
needing shelter mistook the Longstone light.
Hitting the rocks and breaking in two
half the ship sank with passengers and crew.
Some used a lifeboat and others climbed the rocks.
Men, women and bairns were among the lives lost.

Seen from the lighthouse survivors in trouble
Grace and her dad then hauled out their coble.
Then, putting their own lives out on the line
they prayed for strength to reach them in time.
'Gainst wind and waves was a hell of a fight,
almost an hour they fought to stay upright.

Doing their duty and doing what's right
Grace and her dad rowed in the morning light.
Skirting the rocks to keep themselves safe,
They reached survivors, but for some it was too late.
Dad jumped ashore and left Grace with the oars.
She pulled, and she pushed, moving back 'n forth.

Five at a time, more trips would be made.
Only nine plus nine survivors were saved.
William, her dad and one of the crew
rowed back to the rock to collect the last few.

Grace and her mam knew just what to do.
Such a brave young lass at age twenty-two.

Now Grace was a hero like many today
by launching a lifeboat some lives were saved.
Volunteers! No pay, still risking their lives,
yet over the centuries many heroes have died.
So let's not forget all the coxswains and crew,
willing and able to come to our rescue.

The Forfarshire ship was sailing from Hull to Dundee and
mistook the Longstone lighthouse for the Farne Island
lighthouse when seeking shelter from a stormy night. The ship
broke in two. Nine people grabbed a lifeboat. And nine others
made it onto Harcar Rock. The rest of the passengers and crew
were lost. As daylight broke, Grace Darling saw the survivors
on the rocks, and with her dad William, felt it their duty to
save them. With an oar each, they rowed the coble boat for
over an hour. Dad climbed onto the rock to assist with an

injured man while Grace held the boat by rowing back and forth so it didn't smash. The boat only took five at a time, including those who rowed. A woman was holding her two dead children. A crewman and William did the trips while Grace cared for the survivors with her mother. She became a Victorian heroine, and she is a figurehead for the Lifeboat society. Her museum is in Bamburgh, a short walk from the castle. I've also given this poem a song version.

Hartley Pit (Northumberland Mining Disaster January 1862)

Tearful women, staring at the hole
in the January darkness and freezing snow.
Hoping and praying, in vigil waiting
for 204 souls trapped down below.

Volunteers toiled through days and nights,
responding to sounds that the men were alright.
Then on day 3 no sound could be heard.
The rescuers found what they had feared.

For all were asleep and their bodies at peace,
sons with their fathers and brothers embraced.
The gas had been silent and sealed their fate.
The rescuers grieved, they had been too late.

There's always the talk about the men
but communities are built by the women.
Remember the mothers, wives, and sweethearts
whose lives that day had been ripped apart.

"We're going to stay," the women said.
Even though their men were dead,
including their boys aged from 10.
Then, the pit was closed, no work for them.

They prayed to God and asked him why
so many men and youngsters should die.
The answer is plain, new laws would be made.
So that, that sort of thing wouldn't happen again.

The Hartley village coal mine, Hester pit, had one shaft, and above it was a beam-pumping engine removing over 1200 gallons of water a minute.

The beam of the pit's pumping engine broke and fell down the shaft with the rubble trapping the men below. The disaster prompted an immediate change in UK law that required all collieries to have at least two independent means of escape. This accident claimed the lives of 204 people. When the bodies were found, they had all died peacefully from deadly gas. The names on the memorial at St Albans Earsden showed several of the lads were aged 10 to 14.

Lament for My Hometown

Songs of the Northeast of England
full of history, legend, and Lore.
No one today would recognise
there was coal mining, fishing and more.
Neighbours were friendly faces
not distant like today.
Each knew the others business, but
the camaraderie was OK.
Doors open, make yourself at home
'cos we've 'nowt worth nicking.
But even those days are gone.
The terraced streets and cobble stones
with toilets out the back.
Been replaced with little boxes and
Girt big, towering flats.
Some things are better, and vastly improved.
But I'm worried it's my history and culture we'll lose.
Who will remember when I am gone?
The communities ripped by disasters and then reborn.
The strength of the women
and courage of the men.
The widows and orphans.
Well, at least I remember them.

Life in the NE of England

From 14 dad worked as a hewer,
cutting the coal on his knees.
At 17 he joined the navy
for a life of fresh air on the seas.
At 24 they had me, so came back,
to work at Seaham Colliery.
At 30 he trained as a deputy,
then worked with a team of men.
He wouldn't be an Overman,
'Cos that was management back then.
The stuff I remember,
from when I was a kid,
the things that we had
and the things that we did.
Tin bath by the fire and
the netty down the yard.
Living in rented rooms,
the life we lived was hard.
The TV was small about 9 inches square,
it was only black and white, but we didn't care.
We moved to a house in Seaham,
near the Knack pit.
It was much better for me Dad,
because he worked different shifts.

1st shift, back, nights and tub loading,
working round the clock.
The sounds of trucks filled with coal
and trains never stopped.
The toilet was still outside,
this time, just by the back door.
No fitted carpets here,
just rugs on a Lino floor.
Shovelling coal on the fire
and getting a decent blaze,
sometimes we set fire to the chimney!
My goodness! Those were the days.

Dad would pour water on the hot coals
and the steam would make the soot fall.
But only if we got it right,
or else you'd see flames from the chimney at night!
Mrs Ogden on the corner had 20 bairns she'd said.
'Cos in them days ye could only keep warmest in bed.

No one in our street had a phone,
we'd walk to the box by the shops on the road.
The smell of the smoke in the fog,
and soot on the washing if left in the rain.
How fast could we bring it all in and
Yet still have to wash it again!
Now we've got colour TVs and mobile phones
Fast-paced living and fast food to go.
But when my dad retired,
and all the collieries closed.
It was the end of a hard-working era,
No more men, working deep down below.

Lighthouse

I stand here, a silent sentry, sleek and tall.
Seeing everything and saying nothing at all.
I know what you did last night,
in that terrible storm, you put out my light!
I witnessed the crime, that wicked deed
those innocent sailors, your evil greed.
I've saved the life of many a soul
but last night you changed my role.
Not a beacon now, but a treacherous snare.
Unsuspecting victims totally unaware
of the sandbank, hidden out there.
The secret assassin grounding a ship.
Rolling it over and making it sink,
while the wreckers and looters plundered
under cover of waves and thunder.
I'm helpless, unless someone lights me.
A useless tower stuck in the sea.
I need to flash with sweeping arm
warning the sailors and averting harm.
We're dotted around the British Isles
all shapes and sizes and differing styles.
And once, oil or candles lovingly lit,
but now, we're electric, and automatic.

Miner's Daughter

Chorus
I am a miner's daughter, like my mam before.
Like her mam before her,
she worries 'til the menfolk come home.

My youngest brother came off the dole,
He finally agreed to cut the coal.
He's going to join my sisters' men,
He'll be travelling underground with them.
Chorus

Murton Pit, that's where they are.
At seventeen an apprentice he will be.
Training at Vane Tempest where
they cut the coal out underneath the sea.
Chorus

Seaham's siren went one night,
Me dad's at work and so me mam took fright.
The siren sound means anything
from a gas explosion or a roof cave in.
Chorus

Everyone, old miners too
hurried to the pit to hear the news.
Who's still down, who's come out by?
Who's OK and has anybody died?
Chorus

That was not so long ago
The power stations used to use our coal.
But nuclear power has closed the mine,
Me dad an' brothers sign on and stand in line.
Chorus

Derek, my youngest brother, left school and went on the dole. Even our dad did not want him to work down the pit. After a year of no work, he gave in. He actually did his apprenticeship at Seaham Colliery (The Knack) where our dad worked, but it did not fit the song. Derek did go and join my brothers-in-law who worked at Murton. I was going to add a verse about Dawdon Pit too. They were all joined underground anyway. Even up to Ryhope and beyond. The coal field was huge, though some of the seams were a bit thin. My dad said there was still coal to be dug even after they closed the mines after the strikes. It's just that the price wasn't viable. Vane tempest and Dawdon seams went out to sea. Dad took redundancy and retired from The Knack when it closed.

Old News

Chorus
It wasn't in the news today
that doesn't mean it's gone away,
Old news is no news so nothing's changed.
Old news, no news, no nothing's changed.

Throw away people, disposable people.
The poor are increasing their debt.
But they are still people, humans like us.
Is there something we can do, to give them respect?

Chorus
Why save the children, oh what is their future?
Hungry and shot at or pushed to one side.
But they are still children, great is their need.
Is there something we can do, to bring them relief?

Chorus
Albania, Angola, Armenia, Rumania.
Has anyone been there, does anyone care?
Sudan is starving and so many at war.
Is there something we can do, to bring them some peace?
Chorus.

Packed Like Sardines

We're packed like sardines
there's no 9 to 5 here.
I often forget the day of the week
never mind what time of the year.
Nee point putting me lamp on yet
cos there's nowt to see.
'Cept me marra,
who's probbly grinnin at me.
Remembering at the club last night,
he won the darts with a lucky shot.
So now, I owe him a pint.

Down we go, then a sudden jolt
the cable straining the cage has stopped.
It's jammed again, O Flip!
I start to sweat, it's stuffy too,
it juddered and moved up a bit.

And then it dropped like a stone!
Oh God! We're loose; there's summat wrong.
A young lad screamed, A' start to pray.
Am sorry God, look after me, bairns
I won't be home today.
We stopped just short of bottom
someone wet their sel.

Another threw up down me back,
an' me legs had turned to gel.
The air was thick with curses, relief and tears.
'Av' been working this mine for 50 years.
It's happened before.

The bell just rang it lifts again.
This shift is ended; we've had a fright.
We're in no fit state to work tonight.
I bet they dock our wages.
But we'll be back tomorrow
and they'll cram us again in these cages.

I've been reliably told it is highly unlikely the men would
have been given the night off.
They would simply continue down to the working levels and
be expected to carry on.
Minor pit incidents didn't make the news but often affected
the men.

Salt and Pepper Friends

Salt and Pepper came today,
Highlighted hair to hide the grey.
Youthful smiles and laughter lines
now we're retired with busy lives.
To see them I was so pleased
I did a little dance then hugged and squeezed.
We'd finally confirmed a date
and for a change no one was late.
'Twas an afternoon of tea and cake.

We laughed and joked and shared our stories.
Our ups and downs, defeats and glories.
Our aches and pains and medication,
and the years we worked in education.
The pride and joy some students gave,
made the job worthwhile day after day.

Students seen at checkouts and bars,
or pushing prams and driving cars.
Faces remembered, but we forgot names,
the struggles we have with our ageing brains.

When our afternoon was spent,
back home we went, with promises,
to make our visits more frequent.

Seaham Harbour Changes

Chorus
Ring in the changes and ring out tradition,
Bring in the new things and throw out the old.
There's no time to reminisce
you can't stop the progress.
Change for the better, or change for the worse?

Once there was Church Street with the road down the middle
where lorries and cars would travel by day.
Along came the council with their new ideas
and put pots and planters and bricks in the way.

Chorus
Once there were three pits to highlight the skyline,
wheels turned on towers pulling coal from the mines.
Along came the government refusing investment
said our coal is too dear, it's much cheaper abroad.

Chorus
Then there's our coastline it changes each winter.
They built sea defences to keep it at bay.
The cliffs mud and limestone, they can't take the weather,
Each neap tide or storm comes and washes it away.

Chorus
The docks were once busy with coal trucks unloading,
Filling ships holds from the gantries above.
Now they're dismantled, they're no longer needed
There's lorries instead, and it's gravel, wood or stone.

Chorus
Once there was jollity and life in my village.
Once it had a heart like a lion so strong.
Things have been taken, there's nothing replacing,
the changes have come, and the heartbeat has gone.
changes have come, and the heartbeat has gone.

Seaham Harbour is in Co. Durham on the N.E. coastline below Sunderland and above Hartlepool.
Since writing this, many more changes have taken place, and efforts have been made to make Seaham attractive to visitors. It is now well worth a visit.

Terms of Endearment

When I was younger, I'd look through the window
over the hillside and out to the sea.
Thinking about you and wondering where you are,
will you be coming on home back to me?

Chorus
Lover, my love, dearest, beloved.
Will you be coming on home back to me? Repeat

You went to London to go to an interview
said you'd be back as soon as you can.
So I kept waiting and watching out for you
hoping to join you the way that we'd planned.

Chorus
Now I am older, I don't look through windows
Too many houses, they crowd out the sea.
Sometimes I think of you, sometimes I wonder
Will you be coming on home back to me?

Chorus x2

This song was inspired by my coming to live down south.
I left on October 1st, 1971, before my 18th birthday in
December. My parents' house was in Oxford St. off Malvern
Crescent on Deneside at Seaham. We could see the sea

because it was on a hill. The top of the hill is called Mount Pleasant. Coal mining caused many properties to be affected by subsidence. Many houses were removed and years later replaced, but not Oxford St. New housing estates were built when they removed the pit buildings and winding towers. They even landscaped the 'Knack's pit heap beside the Mill Inn bank.

The Cage

"Bye me, love, it's time to go, I'll see yuh in the morning.
Am off to work me bait is packed, the shift'll soon be startin."
Greeting the lads, all hale and hearty, collecting our lamps and kit.
Picking up our tally's, one brass, one zinc.
Brass sez we're on bank, the other sez we're down the pit.
Into the cage packed like sardines, making quite a clatter.
To cover the nerves a bit a banter, and some good-humoured chatter.
Get this bit ower with so we can get to work.
A dinna like this bit, dropping in the dark.
The traverse bell starts ringing
the cage door slams, a lad starts singing.
When we get to the bottom, it's then we take the train
we're cutting the coal from the seam called Low Maine.

As they descend, a sickening jolt and a siren sounds.
Someone swore, silence, no chatter now.
The winch is stuck, the drum has jammed.
Deputy shouts, "Start prayin' lads to God above
or else we'll all be dammed."
A young boy starts to cry, "Hang on, son. It's not our time to die.
Mechanics above'll ge'rit sorted, wu just have to hang here and wait.

Am not ready for hell today, nor to see the pearly gates."
A judder, a shake, a groan, a squeal.
A grinding noise as they turn the wheels.
The sweating men their fists still clenched are glad to see the light.
Foreman sez, "Gan on home lads and have a pint
Be back tomorra when everything's all right."

My brother, Derek said Murton pit had 4 levels, each deck of the cage holding 15 men. 5 on the left and 5 on the right facing each other, then the next unlucky 5 were squeezed in between them. And depending on what they had the night before is what they smelt on the way down. Halitosis, garlic, or beer. As for the smaller lads, they got the lower smells, onions, curries, etc. Then, after the shift, on the way up, they often squeezed in 20 so you couldn't breathe. So, it meant the sweat and smells weren't so bad. (Quoted)

This poem is very loosely based on a true story, which affected my uncle working in the pit. He got panic attacks and anxiety, which affected his heart, and didn't go back down the pit. He and his family were relocated to Yorkshire.

My brother-in-law developed claustrophobia; he also had to stop working down the pit.

The George Elmy Lifeboat

Chorus
Rolling waves can take you
Thunderous waves can break you,
When nothing else can save you.
'Cept a lifeboat and its crew, its crew
a lifeboat and its crew.

Seaham Harbour had a lifeboat
in fact it's had quite a few,
and all of them were volunteers
the Coxswains and the crews.

Chorus
They're designed to be unsinkable
but some then, not like today.
Once they flipped over in the sea
that's often how they would stay.

Chorus
November 1962
George Elmy went to rescue
the fishing coble Economy
off the coast of Dawdon Colliery.

Chorus
Close to the harbour entrance
'gainst waves they had not a chance.
They capsized and lost the crew
and all but one they had rescued

Chorus

Of Seaham Harbour's Lifeboats there have been seven boats, only 1 disaster. And around 287 lives saved; of those, George Elmy had saved 20.

In 1785, the first unsinkable lifeboat was designed and built at South Shields.

Lifeboats started as rowing boats, then sailed, then powered. Although unsinkable, not all were self-righting like today. Heavy stuff below deck and a watertight cabin above. I once lived opposite Mrs Brown, the widow of a lifeboat crew member lost in the disaster at Seaham Harbour. The boat was the George Elmy, a Liverpool-class lifeboat. It was replaced by a Shannon class self-righting lifeboat, the Will and Fanny Kirby, which served from 1963 till 1979. Sunderland and Hartlepool RNLI now cover that coastline.

On the night in question, a fishing coble the Economy, with four men and a boy on board, was struggling in serious storm conditions not far from the harbour, just off Dawdon Colliery. At 4.10pm on 17th November 1962, George Elmy launched. After successfully rescuing the fishermen, she was hit broadside by two 12ft waves at the harbour entrance and capsized. The boat ended upside down on the beach with one survivor clinging to the propeller shaft. The survivor, one of the fishermen, Donald Burrell, lost his brother and his 9yr old son.

The George Elmy went through many lives until it was bought back from a buyer on Ebay. It has been restored to its original condition and is housed in the old Lifeboat station and is a museum of its history and a memorial to the men that lost their lives.

The Graveyard Shift

"Where are ye gannen then Bonny Lad?
dressed all up in yer Sunday best?
But there's no work to be had
for you and the men are being laid to rest."

"Yer face is all washed and clean
and you were laid out straight and fine.
Your Sunday suit hides your broken frame
from the blast that buried you in the mine."

Quietly the town follows the carriage
darkened figures, morose and sad
Wearing their grief like a blanket
Just like they did for yer dad.

Christchurch stands in welcome,
Fresh graves open and waiting
Henry senior, Henry Jr and John
Mrs Bleasdale's whole family is gone.

It's been a year since the blast that took them,
Horses, ponies, boys, and men.
Figures that waited, hoping, now see,
Bonny lad coming to rest in peace.

"Great son, you're found
we can go back underground."
Forlorn figures fading like mist
all Marra's together, on the graveyard shift.

In Seaham, there is an impressive memorial in the Christchurch graveyard for the 26 men and boys that died from an explosion in 1871 at Seaham Colliery.

However, beside it is a smaller, less elaborate monument; perhaps there was less money to pay for it for the 164 men and boys who died in an explosion nine years later, in 1880. 180 horses and ponies also died then, and the last of the men's bodies was recovered a year later. The blast was blamed on a shot-firing accident. My dad was a deputy and shotfirer.

The dead were buried at the same time in two churches. 30 at a time. Some of the headstones had father and sons lost on the same day.

The Miner's Strike 1984/85

Whose fault was it anyway, who was to blame?
They were told the pits were closing,
and that! Was a bloody shame.
Maggie and Scargill with pride on both sides
not giving an inch, so justice denied.
Police in the middle with batons and shields,
our lads had stood firm then left blood in the fields.
The speeches and rallies sounding good to the ears
never touched the misery at home,
nor quelled the wives fears.
Communities were split from the loyalties made,
the family grudges remain to this day.
Soup kitchens and charity supported the men
their wives helping out and encouraging them.
My brother and In-laws were picketing the gates.
My dad escorted in, to make the pit safe.
Despite all the hardship, their cause, it was true,
It didn't break their spirit, they thought victory was sure.
'twas a hard time for everyone,
but they marched singing songs,
and the brass bands kept going, playing along.
Eventually the future, employment and hope
crumbled into dust, just like English coal.

Unknown Warrior

I'm sorry, I didn't know your name
nor for instance, from where you came.
But you did something courageously
you went to war and died for me.
It was your sacrifice that makes us free.
Though you were not the only one
of someone's husband, brother or son.
But you were chosen to come back and tell,
of the dreadful horrors of fighting in hell.
I've seen old photos in brown and white
thousands of you marching away to fight,
then, so few returned, if any.
All the pomp and pageantry
wasn't just for you, but for the many
unknown bodies buried in haste,
the shame of humanity, the senseless waste.
You're laid among kings and statesmen,
maybe a commoner or an Earl's son,
a volunteer, just like everyone.
Giving it all for the king and country.
Preserving our national identity.
You are the Unknown Warrior.